"This bed is too old to sleep in," said Mr Mack.
"I will take it to the tip."

"Let me take the bed,"
said Mrs Mack.
She put the bed on the truck.

Mrs Mack went down the road.

She did not go to the tip.
She went into town.

Mrs Mack took the bed
to the junk shop.

The man in the junk shop gave Mrs Mack some money.

The man in the junk shop put the bed in his shop.

Mrs Mack went home.
"We need a new bed,"
said Mr Mack.

So Mrs Mack took Mr Mack
to the junk shop.

"Look at this bed," said Mr Mack.
He sat on the bed.

"I like this bed," he said.
"This will be a good bed
to sleep in."

Mr Mack gave the junk shop man some money.

He put the bed on the truck.

Mr Mack had a smile.
Mrs Mack had a big smile.

"I will have a good sleep now," said Mr Mack, and he did.